Let the River Flow

T0099877

Let the River Flow

Poetic Praise and Testimonial Tales

Tim Fernandes

WestBow
PRESS
A DIVISION OF THOMAS NELSON

Copyright © 2012 Tim Fernandes

All rights reserved. No part of this book may be used or reproduced by
any means, graphic, electronic, or mechanical, including photocopying,
recording, taping or by any information storage retrieval system
without the written permission of the publisher except in the case
of brief quotations embodied in critical articles and reviews.

WestBow Press books may be ordered through booksellers or by contacting:

WestBow Press
A Division of Thomas Nelson
1663 Liberty Drive
Bloomington, IN 47403
www.westbowpress.com
1-(866) 928-1240

Because of the dynamic nature of the Internet, any web addresses or
links contained in this book may have changed since publication and
may no longer be valid. The views expressed in this work are solely those
of the author and do not necessarily reflect the views of the publisher,
and the publisher hereby disclaims any responsibility for them.

Any people depicted in stock imagery provided by Thinkstock are
models, and such images are being used for illustrative purposes only.

Certain stock imagery © Thinkstock.

ISBN: 978-1-4497-5267-5 (sc)
ISBN: 978-1-4497-5268-2 (hc)
ISBN: 978-1-4497-5266-8 (e)

Library of Congress Control Number: 2012908905

Printed in the United States of America

WestBow Press rev. date: 5/22/2012

OTHER BOOKS BY
TIM FERNANDES

Moon Over Moonachie

Sad Songs and Tattered Tales

To my Mother.

Winifred Iris Fernandes

June 26, 1930 – October 5, 2008,

who was always a shining example to me

of Christ's love.

There is no hope,

nor purpose,

nor true joy,

without Jesus,

our Lord and Savior,

at the center of our lives.

There is more to life......

......than life itself.

Contents

FORWARD

I have not known Tim Fernandes for a long time; we first met in a Christian bookstore some 6 years ago. It was easy to remember him since we both share the same first name. Over time we continued to bump into each other at various school Christmas concerts, Kindergarten promotions, and through local youth sports programs. At each meeting the both of us were happy to stop what we were doing for a cordial "hello, how are you doing?", and then politely move on as casual acquaintances.

We reacquainted ourselves a year and a half ago in the lobby of the church where we both now attend. Since that time our relationship has expanded to more than a casual greeting. These last 18 months we have worshiped, prayed, learned, shared and served together in our local church. In that time I have learned that Tim loves God, his wife, his family, and his church. I have observed a man seeking to know and grow in his relationship with Jesus.

His quiet faithfulness serves as an encouragement to me as I see him as no mere box checker just showing up for Sunday worship or weeknight Bible study. Tim is a man who is seeking to love God with his heart, soul and mind, and learning to love his neighbor as well.

Reading through *Let The River Flow*, I have learned that God has blessed Tim with the ability to pen poems of praise and stories of testimony, to the praise and glory of his Lord and Savior Jesus Christ. His selection of Scripture enhances his writing and serves to minister and encourage. A thoughtful reading of his poetry will bless you as you relate to his prose, while meditating on God's Word.

Understand as you read this, we now have a few things in common. We have both been introduced to Tim Fernandes through a Christian bookstore of some sort. Also, that as you read *Let The River Flow*, you will come to know and appreciate him as I do.

Tim Howard
Associate Pastor
Grace Brethren Church
Simi Valley, California

PREFACE

When I first started writing this book it started out as simply my third book of poetry. It turned out to be so much more. It seemed to take on a life of its own. I realized very quickly that I was merely a tool in this endeavor, that God somehow had a hand in all of this. He was giving the inspiration and words throughout this whole process. Never, in my nearly forty years of writing, have the words come so freely and flowing. I have no other explanation for the book you hold in your hands. All of the glory goes to Him. What had started out as just another book of poetry, became my own personal testimony, my journey with and toward our Almighty God, and Lord and Savior Jesus.

I would also like to acknowledge and thank some people who have both inspired and helped me in my walk of faith. Pastor Dale Whitehead, for his sound Biblical teaching. Lance and Teresa Richards, Wayne and Julie Johnston, Gerry Anderson, the Thrashers, the Arriolas, and all the people at Valley Bible Church, too numerous to mention. Pastors John MacIntosh, Jordan Bakker, and Tim Howard of Grace Brethren Church in Simi Valley, California, for their guidance and knowledge of God's Word. Also of inspiration to me have been the writings of John MacArthur, Charles Stanley, Charles Swindoll, Max Lucado, John Ortberg, C.S.Lewis, and most of all, God's Word, the Bible. And last, but certainly not least, I want to thank my wife Jere for her unending support.

May God's blessings be with you always! Amen.

Tim Fernandes

WHEN ANGELS CRY

(dedicated to Winifred I. Fernandes)

The angels cry out
at the loss that we feel,
they sing of a life
filled with love and devotion,
of kindness and caring
rarely found on this earth,
through struggles and trials,
never faltered or stumbled,
gave of herself
that honored our God,
she has left us behind,
but now has gone home
to be with the Lord,
no more pain and no more suffering,
only joy and peace are hers eternal,
the only solace I find is the joy of knowing
we will be together again someday.

For He shall give His angels charge over you, to keep you in all His ways. In their hands they shall bear you up, lest you dash your foot against a stone.

…..Psalm 91:11-12

Above it stood seraphim; each one had six wings: with two he covered his face, with two he covered his feet, and with two he flew. And one cried to another and said: "Holy, holy, holy is the Lord of hosts; the whole earth is full of His glory!"

…..Isaiah 6:2-3

Tim Fernandes

LET THE RIVER FLOW

Let the river flow till overflowing,
with Your love and majesty,
with Your grace and with Your mercy,
let the river flow.

Let the river flow
through times of trial,
through times of joy and times of peace,
let Your waters cleanse me
with Your spirit,
let the river flow.

Let the river flow
with all Your power,
with Your blood and sacrifice,
to forever wash away my sin,
let your river flow.

And he showed me a pure river of water of life, clear as crystal, proceeding from the throne of God and of the Lamb. In the middle of its street, and on either side of the river, was the tree of life, which bore twelve fruits, each tree yielding its fruit every month. The leaves of the tree were for the healing of the nations.

.....Revelation 22:1-2

"He who believes in Me, as the scripture has said, out of his heart will flow rivers of living water."

.....John 7:38

For thus says the Lord: "Behold, I will extend peace to her like a river, and the glory of the Gentiles like a flowing stream. Then you shall feed; on her sides shall you be carried, and be dandled on her knees."

.....Isaiah 66:12

LIGHT

There is a light that shines through darkness,
there is a light for our despair,
there is a light that has forgiveness,
there is a light that shows He's there,
there is a light to guide our paths,
there is a light to show the way,
there is a light so bright and wonderful,
there is a light to show we're saved,
there is a light that I will long to see
when my days on earth are done,
there is a light, His name is Jesus,
shines down on everyone.

The Lord is my light and my salvation; whom shall I fear? The Lord is the strength of my life; of whom shall I be afraid?

.....Psalm 27:1

The light of the righteous rejoices, but the lamp of the wicked will be put out.

.....Proverbs 13:9

Your word is a lamp to my feet and a light to my path.

.....Psalm 119:105

Then Jesus spoke to them again, saying, "I am the light of the world. He who follows Me shall not walk in darkness, but have the light of life."

.....John 8:12

THE MAN IN THE MIRROR

I can hardly believe the reflection I see,
the man I have become because of You,
Your love and Your mercy
have changed me forever,
barely recognizable
from the person I was,
who is this man I see in the mirror?,
slow to anger,
filled with love,
with desire and longing to help the needy,
share Your gospel to the people around me,
show Your love to a broken world.

Who is this man I see in the mirror?,
not the man I remember
before I was saved.

But be doers of the word, and not hearers only, deceiving yourselves. For if anyone is a hearer of the word and not a doer, he is like a man observing his natural face in a mirror. For he observes himself, goes away, and immediately forgets what kind of man he was.

…..James 1:22-24

But we all, with unveiled face, beholding as in a mirror the glory of the Lord, are being transformed into the same image from glory to glory, just as by the Spirit of the Lord.

…..2 Corinthians 3:18

So God created man in His own image; in the image of God He created him; male and female He created them.

…..Genesis 1:27

BLIND

When I was blind
You gave me sight,
when I was weak
You gave me strength,
throughout my trials
You gave me grace,
in all my anger
You gave me peace,
when I was drowning
You rescued me,
as I lay dying
You gave me life,
for all my sins
You paid the price,
through Your salvation,
no longer blind.

So they again called the man who was blind, and said to him, "Give God the glory! We know that this man is a sinner." He answered and said, "Whether He is a sinner or not I do not know: that though I was blind, now I see."

.....John 9:24-25

"Let them alone. They are blind leaders of the blind. And if the blind leads the blind, both will fall into a ditch."

.....Matthew 15:14

"Woe to you, blind guides, who say,' Whoever swears by the temple, it is nothing; but whoever swears by the gold of the temple; he is obliged to perform it.' "Fools and blind! For which is greater, the gold or the temple that sanctifies the gold?"

.....Matthew 23:16-17

BELIEVE

What will it take

for you to believe?,

when will you wake and realize?,

all that you know

was meant to deceive,

by the one cloaked in darkness,

the father of lies,

will you need to see the waters part?,

or see the mountains move?,

will you need to see a miracle

to bring you to your knees?,

or will you need a revelation

sent from God above?,

amazed by His glory,

His might, and His love.

"He who believes and is baptized will be saved: but he who does not believe will be condemned."

.....Mark 16:16

And truly Jesus did many other signs in the presence of His disciples, which are not written in this book; but these are written that you may believe that Jesus is the Christ, the Son of God, and that believing you may have life in His name.

.....John 20:30-31

You believe that there is one God. You do well. Even the demons believe-and tremble.

.....James 2:19

"For God so loved the world that He gave His only begotten Son, that whoever believes in Him should not perish but have everlasting life."

.....John 3:16

Given The Word

Paula was in one of the most desperate situations of her life, in the midst of a nasty settlement proceeding. She had been divorced for a couple of years, but the property aspect was still not complete. Her ex-husband was an abusive and domineering man, so she was feeling both scared and intimidated by the upcoming hearings.

At the time of her divorce, she was allowed to continue living in the house they had shared as husband and wife, even though it was still in his name, and they had not yet reached an agreement on their joint property. Paula had lived in that house for many years, and the last thing she wanted to do was to move from that house. Besides the inconvenience of having to find a new dwelling, she wanted to keep her daughter in the house she had grown up in, and the school she attended.

To further complicate matters, Paula is a single Mother, who also happens to be legally blind. Moving from that house would be traumatic, since she knew where everything was, and how everything was situated. She also walked to the bus every day to get to work, so a change of this magnitude would be devastating.

We had talked constantly during the course of the trial, and I tried to give her as much support and encouragement as possible. I prayed with her, read scripture, gave her my ear and a shoulder to cry on. Although it was hard to imagine, there was a real chance she could lose the trial, and the house in the process. The trial was not going as well as she had hoped. Her ex-husband was committing perjury on the stand to get the outcome he wanted.

One night during the trial she was particularly distraught over that day's proceedings. She was in tears and emotionally drained. I told her to take a hot bath, read her Bible, pray, and call me later that evening. At the same time, I searched through my Bible trying to find Scripture that would give her hope, strength, and encouragement for the day to come. I found what I thought would be perfect for her situation in the Book of Psalms. I anxiously awaited her call for the opportunity to share those verses with her.

She called me about 10 p.m. that night. A night I will never forget. As I began reading the verses to her, it was unusually quiet on the other end of the line. I continued reading until done with the Scripture I had chosen. There was an eerie silence for a few moments. "Paula, are you there?', I said. Still silence, then she spoke. "I was waiting to see if you were done reading, because I read the exact same verses before I called you".

It was at that moment I realized that God had given us both that Scripture at the exact same time. What an amazing, wonderful feeling it is to know that even through our trials, He is always there to comfort and guide us.

It is You

It is in You, oh Lord,

that I draw my strength,

in these troubled times when I can't go on,

when my body is weary,

when my muscles ache and my heart is heavy,

it is You, oh God,

that shines His light on my darkest days,

and opens my eyes to the wonders about me,

the birds in the morning,

the stars of the night,

the wind through my hair,

the rain on my face;

it is You, my Lord,

I will worship and praise,

when I don't understand the world around me,

or Your purpose and will.

The Lord is my strength and my shield; My heart trusted in Him, and I am helped; Therefore my heart greatly rejoices, and with my song I will praise Him.

.....Psalm 28:7

God is our refuge and strength, a very present help in trouble. Therefore we will not fear, even though the earth be removed, and though the mountains be carried into the midst of the sea; though its waters roar and be troubled, though the mountains shake with its swelling.

.....Psalm 46:1-3

My soul melts from heaviness; strengthen me according to your word. Remove from me the way of lying, and grant me Your law graciously. I have chosen the way of truth; Your judgments I have laid before me.

.....Psalm 119:28-30

Tim Fernandes

FALSE PROPHETS

Beware of false prophets in Armani suits
with trophy wives,
with shiny cars and sold out stadiums,
preaching self-help sermons in the name of God,
who bend and reshape the words of the Bible,
to suit their purpose and lead us astray.

Beware of false prophets
who appeal to the masses,
in widespread telecasts and book signing tours,
more consumed by appearance
than spreading the Word,
more concerned with their ministry,
than feeding the hungry and saving souls.

Beware of false prophets,
the end could be near.

Then I said, "Ah, Lord God! Behold the prophets say to them, 'You shall not see the sword, nor shall you have famine, but I will give you assured peace in this place." And the Lord said to me, "The prophets prophesy lies in My name. I have not sent them, commanded them, nor spoken to them; they prophesy to you a false vision, divination, a worthless thing, and the deceit of their heart. "Therefore thus says the Lord concerning the prophets who prophesy in My name, whom I did not send, and who say, 'Sword and famine shall not be in this land'-'By sword and famine those prophets shall be consumed! "And the people to whom they prophesy shall be cast out in the streets of Jerusalem because of the famine and the sword; they will have no one to bury them-them nor their wives, their sons nor their daughters- for I will pour their wickedness on them.'

.....Jeremiah 14:13-16

ALL THE LOST SOULS

Look all around to the east and the west,
on the highways and byways,
on streets and in subways,
a man with a shopping cart,
clothes tattered and torn,
children starving and homeless in shelters and alleys,
a woman haunted by the cry of an unborn child.

Look all around you in small towns and big cities,
at all the lost souls wandering and forgotten,
unaware of a God who loves and adores them,
who longs for His people to show them the way,
to embrace and comfort in the name of Jesus.

Take a look all around you;
and see the lost souls.

"My people have been lost sheep, their shepherds have led them astray; they have turned them away on the mountains. They have gone from mountain to hill; they have forgotten their resting place.

.....Jeremiah 50:6

"What do you think? If a man has a hundred sheep, and one of them goes astray, does he not leave the ninety-nine and go to the mountains to seek the one that is straying? "And if he should find it, assuredly, I say to you, he rejoices more over that sheep than over the ninety-nine that did not go astray. Even so it is not the will of your Father who is in heaven that one of these little ones should perish."

.....Matthew 18:12-14

Tim Fernandes

A PERFECT LOVE

All my life I have searched
and have sought a perfect love,
someone to hold me,
tell me I'm cherished
and loved like no other,
to know my heart and feel my pain,
accept me for the person I am,
to share my joy
and share my sorrow,
only to find it was there all along,
given to me before I was born,
at a price so high
I can never repay,
the love of my Savior on Calvary;
a perfect love.

Your mercy, O Lord, is in the heavens; Your faithfulness
reaches to the clouds.

.....Psalm 36:5

How precious is Your lovingkindness, O God! Therefore the
children of men put their trust under the shadow of Your
wings.

.....Psalm 36:7

He loves righteousness and justice; the earth is full of the
goodness of the Lord.

.....Psalm 33:5

For Your mercy reaches unto the heavens, and Your truth unto
the clouds.

.....Psalm 57:10

Because Your lovingkindness is better than life, my lips shall
praise You.

.....Psalm 63:3

Tim Fernandes

ONE ACT OF KINDNESS

One act of kindness is all it will take
to change this world for the better,
show His love to the worn and the weary,
imagine each person
a reflection of Christ.

One word of caring is all it will take
to ease the pain of the lost and suffering,
show His grace to the battered and broken,
imagine each person
extending a hand.

One shoulder to cry on is all it will take
to comfort people in need and despair,
show His mercy to widows and orphans,
imagine each person
living His word.

He who despises his neighbor sins; but he who has mercy on the poor, happy is he.

.....Proverbs 14:21

He who oppresses the poor reproaches his Maker, but he who honors Him has mercy on the needy.

.....Proverbs 14:31

He who has pity on the poor lends to the Lord, and He will pay back what he has given.

.....Proverbs 19:17

But the fruit of the Spirit is love, joy, peace, longsuffering, kindness, goodness, faithfulness, gentleness, self-control. Against such there is no law.

.....Galatians 5:22-23

And be kind to one another, tenderhearted, forgiving one another, even as God in Christ forgave you.

.....Ephesians 4:32

Saying Goodbye

I currently live in sunny California, but was born and bred in suburban New Jersey. Once a year I make an exodus there to visit my family. I usually make my reservations at the last minute, but on this particular visit, my wife and I made reservations well in advance of our trip, about six months in advance, in fact.

Our visit was scheduled for early September, but during the course of the summer I learned that my mother's health was on the decline. She was losing weight at an alarming rate, despite eating normally.

On the week that we arrived in New Jersey, my mother had scheduled a doctor's appointment to try to determine why she was losing so much weight. The results of her tests showed that she had stomach cancer, and she would have to start chemo and radiation treatments immediately. My visit was not going as I expected, to say the least. Most of my time in New Jersey was spent taking my mom to doctor's visits and treatments. However, I was thankful that I was able to be there in her time of need.

As my time there came to an end, I left with hope and prayer that through treatments and God's grace, my mother would be healed. I checked in constantly with my mother during that month to see how she was faring with her treatments. It was taking a toll on her. She was a frail little lady, and was tired and weak most of the time.

Then came a phone call in late September from my sister. My mom had gone to sleep the night before, but in essence was not waking up. She was breathing and alive, but not coherent or responding to anyone or anything. She was taken to the hospital that morning and admitted. The week that ensued was absolute torture for me. I was 3,000 miles away, and helpless to do anything.

I called my sister repeatedly to get updates on my mom's condition. For that entire week my mother was in a comatose state, not responding to anything. There was no sign of improvement whatsoever. I remember being so unsure of what to do, if anything.

Then I heard a voice, not an audible voice, but a voice from within telling me in no uncertain terms that I needed to book a flight to New Jersey that weekend. It was a moment I can't really explain, but I listened to that voice, nonetheless.

I flew to New Jersey on Saturday, October 5th, and arrived at about 6 p.m. My son was waiting at the airport to pick me up, and we immediately drove to the hospital. When we arrived it was close to 7 p.m., and my two daughters were in my mother's room waiting for us. I stood by my mother's side, held her hand, told her I was there, and that I loved her. I am not sure if she heard me at all. She was still not responding to anything.

My children and I were in the room for about an hour, when I noticed that my mother's breathing pattern had changed. It had become shorter and more labored. It wasn't long before her breathing had completely stopped. She was gone.

I was her firstborn. As she was there when I took my first breathe, I was there as she took her last, and left us to be with the Lord.

It was an amazing display of God's sovereignty and grace. His perfect timing, in allowing me to not only be there in her time of need, but also to say goodbye.

THE FINAL CUT

When all is done
and the last breathe is taken,
when earthly ties exist no more,
when you pass from this life
through the gates of Heaven,
and stand before His throne,
when He looks into the Book of Life
and your works and deeds are weighed,
as your name appears upon those pages
and you know that you are saved,
an eternity of joy awaits,
not eternity of pain,
imagine the pomp and jubilation
when you make the final cut.

Riches do not profit in the day of wrath, but righteousness delivers from death.

.....Proverbs 11:4

Therefore the ungodly shall not stand in the judgment, nor sinners in the congregation of the righteous. For the Lord knows the way of the righteous, but the way of the ungodly shall perish.

.....Psalm 1:5-6

But why do you judge your brother? Or why do you show contempt for your brother? For we shall all stand before the judgment seat of Christ. For it is written: "As I live, says the Lord, every knee shall bow to Me, and every tongue shall confess to God." So then each of us shall give account of himself to God.

.....Romans 14:10-12

Tim Fernandes

THE PRIDE OF HIS KINGDOM

Blessed are the children,

the pride of His kingdom,

fragile and helpless,

precious and frail,

we are called to protect,

nurture and feed them,

a calling from God unheard and unheeded,

so many are starving and yet we do nothing,

so many are dying because we don't care,

no clean water to drink,

no food on the table,

so many alone to fend for themselves,

how can we sleep in comfort and conscience?,

when the pride of His kingdom is hurting and wanting,

when our plates are full

and our lives are blessed.

But Jesus called them to Him and said, "Let the little children come to Me, and do not forbid them; for of such is the kingdom of God. "Assuredly, I say to you, whoever does not receive the kingdom of God as a little child will by no means enter it."

…..Luke 18:16-17

"If you then, being evil, know how to give good gifts to your children, how much more will your Father who is in heaven give good things to those who ask Him!

…..Matthew 7:11

At that time Jesus answered and said, "I thank You, Father, Lord of heaven and earth, that You have hidden these things from the wise and prudent and have revealed them to babes.

…..Matthew 11:25

Train up a child in the way he should go, and when he is old he will not depart from it

…..Proverbs 22:6

Tim Fernandes

WHEN HE RETURNS

When nation fights nation
and false prophets rise,
when countries fall and all seems lost,
angels will descend on earth to battle Satan's horde,
and cast them to a fiery pit to live forevermore,
the winds will rise
and from the clouds appear,
Christ in all His glory,
where earth and heaven meet,
a new Earth, a new Heaven, a new Jerusalem;
evil will be conquered,
joy and peace prevail,
with Jesus as our Lord and King of all the universe;
when He returns.

Therefore, since all these things will be dissolved, what manner of persons ought you to be in holy conduct and godliness, looking for and hastening the coming of the day of God, because of which the heavens will be dissolved, being on fire, and the elements will melt with fervent heat? Nevertheless we, according to His promise, look for new heavens and a new earth in which righteousness dwells.

.....2 Peter 3:11-13

"But in those days, after that tribulation, the sun will be darkened, and the moon will not give its light; the stars of heaven will fall, and the powers in the heavens will be shaken. Then they will see the Son of Man coming in the clouds in great power and glory. And then He will send His angels, and gather together His elect from the four winds, from the farthest part of earth to the farthest part of heaven."

.....Mark 13:24-27

Then I saw another sign in heaven, great and marvelous; seven angels having the seven last plagues, for in them the wrath of God is complete

.....Revelation 15:1

For the Lord himself will descend from heaven with a shout, with the voice of an archangel, and with the trumpet of God. And the dead in Christ will rise first.

.....1 Thessalonians 4:16

Tim Fernandes

TREASURES

What is our treasure?,

where does it lie?,

in the homes that we own or the cars that we drive ?,

in the jobs that we go to ?,

the promotions we strive ?,

our big screen t.v.'s and video games ?,

our manicured lawns and vacations abroad ?,

or does it lie with family and friends?,

in spreading the Gospel

and showing Christ's love ?;

where we find our hearts dwelling,

we will find our treasure.

"Do not lay up for yourselves, treasures on earth, where moth and rust destroy and where thieves break in and steal; but lay up for yourselves treasures in heaven, where neither moth nor rust destroys and where thieves do not break in and steal. For where your treasure is, there your heart will be also."

.....Matthew 6:19-21

Wisdom and knowledge will be the stability of your times, and the strength of salvation; the fear of the Lord is His treasure.

.....Isaiah 33:6

That their hearts may be encouraged, being knit together in love, and attaining to all riches of the full assurance of understanding, to the knowledge of the mystery of God, both of the Father and of Christ, in whom are hidden all the treasures of wisdom and knowledge.

.....Colossians 2:2-3

40 DAYS AND 40 NIGHTS

For 40 days and 40 nights God flooded the earth,
with torrential rain to wash away sin,
entrusting Noah with a new beginning,
a life of worship for all mankind.

For 40 days and 40 nights Christ walked through the desert,
tested and tempted by Satan's lies,
prepared for His ministry through fasting and prayer,
to die on a cross and be risen again.

For 40 days and 40 nights God shaped and restored me,
healed me of cancer,
my purpose was shown,
through His grace and His mercy,
through His Word was reborn.

In the six hundredth year of Noah's life, in the second month, the seventeenth day of the month, on that day all the fountains of the great deep were broken up, and the windows of heaven were opened. And the rain was on the earth forty days and forty nights.

.....Genesis 7:11-12

So God blessed Noah and his sons, and said to them, "Be fruitful and multiply, and fill the earth."

.....Genesis 9:1

Then Jesus was led up by the Spirit into the wilderness to be tempted by the devil. And when He had fasted for forty days and forty nights, afterward He was hungry. Now when the tempter came to Him, he said, "If you are the Son of God, command that these stones become bread." But He answered and said, "It is written, Man shall not live by bread alone, but by every word that proceeds from the mouth of God." Then the devil took Him up into the holy city, set Him on the pinnacle of the temple, and said to Him, "If you are the Son of God throw Yourself down. For it is written: 'He shall give His angels charge over you,' and, 'In their hands they shall bear you up, lest you dash your foot against a stone.' Jesus said to him, "It is written again, 'You shall not tempt the Lord your God.'"

.....Matthew 4:1-7

Tim Fernandes

FAIR-WEATHER CHRISTIANS

Church every Sunday,
but when Monday arrives,
all is forgotten,
work has begun,
business takes over,
the rush and the grind,
problems and clutter take over our lives;
what was read from the Bible,
faded and gone,
songs sung of worship just a memory now;
will we follow His Word?,
live it day by day?,
or be fair-weather Christians
leaving Sunday behind?

Exalt the Lord our God, and worship at His footstool-He is holy.

.....Psalm 99:5

Therefore the Lord said: Inasmuch as these people draw near with their mouths and honor Me with their lips, but have removed their hearts far from Me, and their fear toward Me is taught by the commandment of men.

.....Isaiah 29:13

Take words with you, and return to the Lord, say to Him, "Take away all iniquity; receive us graciously, for we will offer the sacrifices of our lips.

.....Hosea 14:2

"These people draw near to Me with their mouth, and honor Me with their lips, but their heart is far from Me. And in vain they worship Me, teaching as doctrines the commandments of men."

.....Matthew 15:8-9

ANSWER TO A PRAYER

On an unforgettable night in July of 2005, my daughter Carly had gotten very ill. She was vomiting and couldn't keep anything down. She was 1 ½ years old at the time, and at worst her mother and I thought it was some kind of stomach virus. However, her condition continued into the following day, and was becoming a great concern, to say the least. We decided to take her to the doctor the next day, seeing as though she was in danger of dehydration.

The doctor had come to the same conclusion as us, that Carly has some form of virus, and prescribed pedialyte to help with her dehydration.

On the following day she seemed slightly better. She was drinking the pedialyte and keeping it down, but still had no appetite for anything else. I vividly remember holding her on my lap, and noticing that her breathing was abnormal. Something just didn't seem right to me, and I expressed this feeling to her mom. It was at that point we decided to take Carly to the hospital for further examination.

It turned out to be a grueling, fear filled day for us. After many hours of tests and examination, the doctors still couldn't figure out what was ailing her. By that evening, the doctors finally decided to transfer Carly to the children's unit in Los

Angeles, where she could get better care, and a better chance of finding out exactly what was wrong with her.

When we arrived at the children's unit, they immediately brought her to the Intensive Care Unit.

After what seemed like an eternity, but was probably closer to an hour in reality, it was determined that my daughter's pancreas had stopped functioning properly, and had stopped producing insulin to her body. My little girl was a type1 diabetic, but far worse was the immediate danger she was in. Her blood sugar level was dangerously high, and she wasn't getting any nutrients. She was now in real danger.

They needed to get an IV into her as soon as possible to keep her stable. I can't say enough about how dedicated and caring the nurses and doctors were in the ICU, hovering over and tending to Carly's every need. But as hard as they tried, they could not get an IV into Carly's tiny veins.

After approximately two hours of trying without success, it was decided to call a specialist in. Unfortunately, the specialist was two hours away in Santa Barbara. Carly's life was hanging in the balance, and all we could do was wait and pray.

The specialist finally arrived about two hours later, and they wheeled Carly into another room, where they would attempt once again to get the IV in with the aid of the specialist. We waited patiently outside that door for news that the IV was in, and that Carly could begin her recovery.

Suddenly the door swung open. The doctor approached us, but the news was not good. Even the specialist was having a hard time getting the shunt in. He told us he was going to try one more time, and if unsuccessful, would have to surgically insert it. I knew that every wasted moment brought my daughter closer to death, and I was helpless to do anything about it.

As the doctor was in there, trying once more to get the shunt in, we suddenly got a call on our cell phone. It was one of the pastors from our church. He had heard from one of our friends the danger Carly was in. We told him what the current situation was, and asked if he could pray with us. We all prayed together for a few minutes, and then, almost immediately after we had prayed, the door swung open. It was the doctor with the great news that he was able to get the IV in, and Carly could now stabilize, and begin to improve.

On that unforgettable day, God answered our prayers, and showed me what a mighty and merciful God He truly is.

THIS FALLEN EARTH

How do I begin to show a love like Yours?,
how do I reach others to show them Your grace?,
this is my calling and this is my purpose,
to be an example to the people around me,
to spread Your Word to the lost and broken,
to shine Your light on a dreary day.

Surely anger and despair have overcome me,
so incensed by the darkness and wrongs of this world,
I want to turn over tables like Christ in the temple,
shout to You, Lord, at the top of my lungs;
give me patience and mercy to be my guide,
as I reach out to others on this fallen earth.

For you, brethren, have been called to liberty; only do not use liberty as an opportunity for the flesh, but through love serve one another. For all the law is fulfilled in one word, even in this; "You shall love your neighbor as yourself.'

…..Galatians 5:13-14

And we know that all things work together for good to those who love God, to those who are the called according to His purpose. For whom He foreknew, He also predestined to be conformed to the image of His Son, that He might be the first-born among many brethren. Moreover whom He predestined, these He also called; whom He called, these He also justified; and whom He justified, these He also glorified.

…..Romans 8:2

Now the Passover of the Jews was at hand, and Jesus went up to Jerusalem. And He found in the temple those who sold oxen and sheep and doves, and the money changers do-ing business. When He had made a whip of cords, He drove them all out of the temple, with the sheep and the oxen, and poured out the changers' money and overturned the tables. And He said to those who sold doves, "Take these things away! Do not make my Father's house a house of merchan-dise!"

…..John 2:13-16

Tim Fernandes

AMERICA

America the beautiful,

America the proud,

the land of the plentiful,

the land of the blessed,

resources wasted through disposable living,

families shattered and torn by divorce and abandonment,

sex sold daily on billboards and television,

prayer taken from classrooms in the name of freedom,

"In God we trust" the foundation it's built on,

removed from currency,

from buildings and courtrooms,

the Commandments of God discarded and forgotten,

worshipping idols of wealth and possessions;

America the lost,

America the greedy,

where will you be when the Lord comes again?

How long, O you sons of men, will you turn My glory to shame? How long will you love worthlessness and seek false-hood?

…..Psalm 4:2

Let us hear the conclusion of the whole matter: fear God and keep His commandments, for this is man's all. For God will bring every work into judgment, including every secret thing, whether good or evil.

…..Ecclesiastes 12:13-14

The wicked shall be turned into hell, and all the nations that forget God. For the needy shall not always be forgotten; the expectation of the poor shall not perish forever.

…..Psalm 9:17-18

Tim Fernandes

HALLELUJAH

When I wake in the morning,

as a new day dawns,

I will sing hallelujah,

for the Lord is good;

all He has given are blessings unearned;

when troubles arise and trials begin,

I will shout hallelujah,

thank Him and praise Him,

be content with my lot;

when overwhelmed by frustration,

be still and in prayer,

ask for forgiveness,

for guidance and peace;

when my world falls apart and I lose all control,

I will cry hallelujah,

for the Lord is with me to show me the way.

After these things I heard a loud voice of a great multitude in heaven, saying, "Alleluia! Salvation and glory and honor and power belong to the Lord our God! "For true and righteous are His judgments, because He has judged the great harlot who corrupted the earth with her fornication; and He has avenged on her the blood of His servants shed by her."

…..Revelation 19:1-2

My brethren, count it all joy when you fall into various trials, knowing that the testing of your faith produces patience. But let patience have its perfect work, that you may be perfect and complete, lacking nothing.

…..James 1:2-4

A fool vents all his feelings, but a wise man holds them back.

…..Proverbs 29:11

Therefore by Him let us continually offer the sacrifice of praise to God, that is, the fruit of our lips, giving thanks to His name.

…..Hebrews 13:15

SECOND CHANCE

When I think of the things
that I have done,
the anger and hurt
that consumed and controlled me,
the pride and jealousy that filled my soul,
the sin that engulfed me
like a raging fire;
I fall to my knees and thank the Lord,
I stop and remember my second chance;
given by grace,
given by love,
given by an almighty God;
His only Son
was crucified to wash me clean,
the price that He paid
for my second chance.

Who can understand his errors? Cleanse me from secret faults.
Keep back Your servant also from presumptuous sins; let
them not have dominion over me. Then shall I be blameless,
and I shall be innocent of great transgression.

…..Psalm 19:12-13

"To Him all the prophets witness that, through His name,
whoever believes in Him will receive remission of sins."

…..Acts 10:43

In Him we have redemption through His blood, the forgive-
ness of sins, according to the riches of His grace which He
made to abound toward us in all wisdom and prudence.

…..Ephesians 1:7-8

He has delivered us from the power of darkness and con-
veyed us into the kingdom of the Son of His love, in whom
we have redemption through His blood, the forgiveness of
sins.

…..Colossians 1:13-14

COMPREHEND

No matter how hard I try to imagine,
I can't comprehend
how mighty and awesome You are,
my God,
the maker of the universe,
creator of all things;
flowers that bloom in springtime,
leaves that turn in autumn,
the colors and shadows at twilight,
the brilliance of the sun at dawn,
the majesty of mountains,
the vastness of the seas,
surrounding us with beauty
everywhere we turn;
we only need to open our eyes,
to see Your glory
and try to comprehend.

He has made everything beautiful in its time. Also He has put
eternity in their hearts, except that no one can find out the
work that God does from beginning to end.

…..Ecclesiastes 3:11

One thing I have desired of the Lord, that I will seek: that I
may dwell in the house of the Lord all the days of my life, to
behold the beauty of the Lord, and to inquire in His temple.

…..Psalm 27:4

In the beginning God created the heavens and the earth. The
earth was without form, and void; and darkness was on the
face of the deep. And the Spirit of God was hovering over the
face of the waters.

…..Genesis 1:1-2

Praise Him, sun and moon; praise Him, all you stars of light!
Praise Him, you heavens of heavens, and you waters above
the heavens! Let them praise the name of the Lord, for He
commanded and they were created. He also established them
forever and ever; He made a decree which shall not pass
away.

…..Psalm 148:3-6

Death Sentence Waived

It had been almost one year since my youngest child, Carly had been born. She was truly a blessing, but quite a surprise, nonetheless. I was 53 years old at the time, and the last thing I ever expected was to become a father again. Carly's mother and I had discussed on several occasions the possibility of me getting a vasectomy. It was a decision I was putting off for almost a year, but finally agreed to see a doctor, and at the very least discuss it. During the course of my examination there was discovered what the doctor called "a small nodule".

After my checkup was complete, the doctor told me he would like to schedule a biopsy as soon as possible. At this point I was getting a little concerned, and certainly not looking forward to that procedure. In spite of my feelings, I knew it was necessary to find out what that nodule was.

I had the biopsy about a week later, and then another week's wait to learn the results of the test. I will never forget the emotions that flooded through me when the doctor told me I had prostate cancer. The doctor proceeded to explain that the cancer was in a very early stage, and the options I had for treatment. My choices were radiation and chemotherapy treatments or surgically removing the prostate gland altogether. Of course, this was not an easy choice to make. I had to think and pray about it for a few days.

The cancer was in its early stages, and was believed to be confined to the prostate with no sign of spreading. There were no guarantees for either treatment, but I felt my best chance for survival was with the surgery, as opposed to the chemo-radiation treatments.

I went in for my surgery on April 13th, 2004. You tend to remember dates like that. Life changing dates. I recall lying on the gurney as the doctors and nurses shaved me, gave me anesthetics, and prepared me for surgery. I prayed to our God to see me through, that I could once again see my little daughter, but at the same time, I was at peace with the prospect of not making it, and joining Him in heaven, if that be His will.

I came out of the anesthesia in my hospital room, and now have a deep understanding and appreciation of what it is like for women who have c-sections at childbirth. The first few hours of recovery were pretty surreal. All had gone well with the surgery. The doctor had removed the prostate successfully, and there were no signs that the cancer had spread. Hallelujah, I was cancer free! I was feeling pretty blessed at that point, especially when I learned that there was another patient on my ward that had prostate cancer as well, but in his case, they didn't catch it in time. For reasons unknown to me, God had chosen to spare me, and give me a second chance.

On the day of my surgery, as I was recovering in my room, Carly's mom came to visit me. She brought me a copy of Rick Warren's "A Purpose Driven Life" to read as I healed from my surgery.

The first week of recovery was pretty grueling. I had to get up and walk around to get my muscles healed and working again. I remember vividly just how painful it was to do that.

I was in the hospital four days altogether. Upon release, my days were spent resting on the sofa, reading my Bible, getting up periodically to work my muscles back into shape, emptying my cafiter, and reading a chapter of "A Purpose Driven Life" each day. I must admit, after about a week of this, I was going a little stir crazy. I couldn't wait to be completely healed, and get back to work. But that was out of my control, and in the hands of God and my doctor.

So I waited patiently, absorbing God's Word and in prayer daily. After exactly forty days, I was finally released by my doctor to return to work. God had used that forty days to heal me both physically and spiritually, to give me His Word, and show me His purpose through the Bible, and that book.

God, in His amazing grace and mercy, had given me a second chance.

JOHN 4,7
JESUS AT THE WELL WITH WOMAN FROM SAMARIA

OF WHORES AND ANGELS

The redeemed and the fallen,

the broken and saved,

whores and angels and sinners and saints,

jews and gentiles and fishers of men,

children and lepers,

the demon possessed,

a samaritan woman,

the crippled and dead,

Lazarus risen,

the thief on the cross,

a tax collector who followed His call.

All touched by Jesus,

by His mercy and grace,

all loved by Jesus;

forever changed.

When they had crossed over, they came to the land of Gennesaret. And when the men of that place recognized Him, they sent out into all that surrounding region, brought to Him all who were sick, and begged Him that they might only touch the hem of His garment. And as many as touched it were made perfectly well.

----Matthew 14:34-36

Now when He had said these things, He cried in a loud voice, "Lazarus, come forth!" And he who had died came out bound hand and foot with grave-clothes, and his face was wrapped with a cloth. Jesus said to them, "Loose him, and let him go."

.....John 11:43-44

And as He walked by the Sea of Galilee, He saw Simon and Andrew his brother casting a net into the sea; for they were fishermen. Then Jesus said to them, "Follow Me, and I will make you become fishers of men." They immediately left their nets and followed Him.

.....Mark 1:16-18

Tim Fernandes

BLESSED

Blessed is the man who has lost it all,
stripped of pride and false beliefs,
no more barriers,
no more chains,
free to see clearly with unclouded eyes,
free to hear clearly the voice of God.

Blessed is the man who has lost it all,
the door is opened for a greater calling,
no more delusions of self-importance,
no value put on possessions and wealth.

Blessed is the man who has lost it all,
the way has been made to be drawn to the Lord.

Blessed is the man who walks not in the counsel of the ungodly, nor stands in the path of sinners, nor sits in the seat of the scornful; but his delight is in the law of the Lord, and in His law he meditates day and night.

-----Psalm 1:1-2

Blessed is he whose transgression is forgiven, whose sin is covered. Blessed is the man to whom the Lord does not impute iniquity, and in whose spirit there is no deceit.

-----Psalm 32:1-2

Blessed are the poor in spirit, for theirs is the kingdom of heaven. Blessed are those who mourn, for they shall be comforted. Blessed are the meek, for they shall inherit the earth. Blessed are those who hunger and thirst for righteousness, for they shall be filled. Blessed are the merciful, for they shall obtain mercy. Blessed are the pure in heart, for they shall see God. Blessed are the peacemakers, for they shall be called sons of God. Blessed are those who are persecuted for righteousness' sake, for theirs is the kingdom of heaven.

-----Matthew 5:3-10

Tim Fernandes

IT'S TIME

It's time for me to step out of the boat,
it's time for me to walk on the water,
it's time for me to trust in the Lord,
to know that He holds me and won't let me fall,
it's time for me to praise and extol Him,
share His Word and love to the people around me,
it's time for me to be a living example,
a reflection of being a believer in Christ,
it's time for me to live fully in faith,
to know that He guides me through trials and strife.

And Peter answered Him and said, "Lord, if it is You, command me to come to You on the water." So He said, "Come." And when Peter had come down out of the boat, he walked on the water to go to Jesus. But when he saw that the wind was boisterous, he was afraid; and beginning to sink he cried out, saying, "Lord, save me!" And immediately Jesus stretched out His hand and caught him, and said to him, "O you of little faith, why did you doubt?"

…...Matthew 14:28-31

Trust in the Lord with all your heart, and lean not on your own understanding; in all your ways acknowledge Him, and He shall direct your paths.

…...Proverbs 3:5-6

I will bless the Lord at all times; His praise shall continually be in my mouth. My soul shall make its boast in the Lord; the humble shall hear of it and be glad. Oh, magnify the Lord with me, and let us exalt His name together.

…...Psalm 34:1-3

The Lord will guide you continually, and satisfy your soul in drought, and strengthen your bones; you shall be like a watered garden, and like a spring of water, whose waters do not fail.

…...Isaiah 58:11

Tim Fernandes

RISE ABOVE

(dedicated to T4)

When gossip and unkindness filter through our lives,
when governments and politics endorse a fallen world,
when advertisements and television reflect a life of sin,
when disillusionment and anger take control of me,
I will rise above it and turn the other way;
and focus on God's Word.

When Satan's work is all around us,
and evil lurks at every turn,
when all has crumbled and life seems lost,
I will rise above it and run the other way,
I will set my eyes on Christ and the wonder of the cross;
I will rise above.

Do not marvel at this; for the hour is coming in which all who are in the graves will hear His voice and come forth-those who have done good, to the resurrection of life, and those who have done evil, to the resurrection of condemnation.

-----John 5:28-29

You have become estranged from Christ, you who attempt to be justified by law; you have fallen from grace.

-----Galatians 5:4

For I fear lest, when I come, I shall not find you such as I wish, and that I shall be found by you such as you do not wish; lest there be contentions, jealousies, outbursts of wrath, selfish ambitions, backbitings, whisperings, conceits, tumults; lest, when I come again, my God will humble me among you, and I shall mourn for many who have sinned before and have not repented of the uncleanness, fornication, and lewdness which they have practiced.

-----2 Corinthians 12:20-21

Do not quench the Spirit. Do not despise prophecies. Test all things; hold fast what is good. Abstain from every form of evil.

-----1 Thessalonians 5:19-22

ASHAMED

I will not be ashamed to proclaim Your name,
to the people I meet,
to the world around me.

I will not be afraid through the darkest of storms,
through trials and pain,
through fire and rain You are always with me.

I will not be timid to share the Gospel,
to tell of Your love and the price that You paid.

I will not hold back from telling Your story,
of redemption and glory,
of promise and praise;
I will not be ashamed.

"For whoever is ashamed of Me and My words, of him the Son of Man will be ashamed when He comes in His own glory, and in His Father's, and of the holy angels."

-----Luke 9:26

For I am not ashamed of the gospel of Christ, for it is the power of God to salvation for everyone who believes, for the Jew first and also for the Greek. For in it the righteousness of God is revealed from faith to faith; as it is written, "The just shall live by faith."

-----Romans 1:16-17

Therefore do not be ashamed of the testimony of our Lord, nor of me His prisoner, but share with me in the sufferings for the gospel according to the power of God, who has saved us and called us with a holy calling, not according to our works, but according to His own purpose and grace which was given to us in Christ Jesus before time began.

-----2 Timothy 1:8-9

Tim Fernandes

ONE MORE STEP FROM EDEN

Every step we take is one more step from Eden,
with every broken marriage and each new abortion,
with every lonely senior and each abused child;
a further step away.

Every step we take is one more step from Eden,
with each starving family and every homeless person,
with each child abduction and fallen politician,
with each war that's fought and every genocide;
a further step away.

Every step we take is one more step from Eden,
with each gossip spoken and angry tongue unleashed,
every time we turn our backs on the hurting and the needy;
one more step from Eden.

The Lord planted a garden eastward in Eden, and there He put the man whom He had formed. And out of the ground the Lord God made every tree grow that is pleasant to the sight and good for food. The tree of life was also in the midst of the garden, and the tree of the knowledge of good and evil.

…..Genesis 2:8-9

Then the Lord God took the man and put him in the garden of Eden to tend and keep it. And the Lord God commanded the man, saying, "Of every tree of the garden you may freely eat, but of the tree of the knowledge of good and evil you shall not eat, for in the day that you eat of it you shall surely die."

…..Genesis 2:15-17

OH WHAT MYSTERY

Oh what mystery,
the works of Your hands
and the gifts You have given,
how You know me and love me
despite my transgressions.

Oh what mystery,
each breath that is given to live a new day,
how the Spirit indwells
to strengthen and guide us.

Oh what mystery,
each sunrise and sunset's splendor and beauty,
how You hold the universe
in the palm of Your hand.

In Him we have redemption through His blood, the forgiveness of sins, according to the riches of His grace which He made to abound toward us in all wisdom and prudence, having made known to us the mystery of His will, according to His good pleasure which He purposed in Himself.

.....Ephesians 1:7-9

But we speak the wisdom of God in a mystery, the hidden wisdom which God ordained before the ages for our glory.

.....1 Corinthians 2:7

CONCLUSION

I wanted to conclude my book with a thank you and a prayer. First of all, I thank you for purchasing this book. In doing so, you have supported a few causes close and dear to my heart. A portion of the proceeds from the sale of this book will go to benefit children in need through World Vision, the mission work of Grace Brethren Church in Simi Valley, California, as well as JDRF (Juvenile Diabetes Research Foundation), and Imagineacure.

Secondly, my prayer is that in some small way, I have, through my writings, been able to minister to you in your walk of faith. That is, and was the driving force and purpose I envisioned for this book.

All the power, and glory, and honor to Him.

----Amen.

NOTES

Tim Fernandes

NOTES

NOTES

NOTES

NOTES

Tim Fernandes

NOTES

NOTES

Tim Fernandes

NOTES

NOTES

Tim Fernandes

NOTES

NOTES

Tim Fernandes

NOTES

NOTES

Tim Fernandes

NOTES

NOTES

Tim Fernandes

NOTES

NOTES

NOTES

NOTES

Tim Fernandes

NOTES

NOTES